MUMBLINGS

The Inspirational Poetry
of
Joseph Hoey

Author
1999

Dear Barb:

The Betty in the back of this
book is me. I Thought
you would enjoy the
mumblings of my friend
Joe. The Mary
is our Mary.
love
B.

Copyright © 1999 by Joseph Hoey

ISBN 0-7414-0101-0

Published by:
Buy Books on the web.com
862 West Lancaster Avenue
Bryn Mawr, PA 19010-3222
Info@buybooksontheweb.com
www.buybooksontheweb.com
Toll-free (877) BUYBOOK

Printed in the United States of America

Printed on Recycled Paper

Published March-1999

Dedication

This collection of poetry is lovingly dedicated to the four people who have given meaning to my life. First, my mother and father, Alberta and Joe, who though now deceased, filled my life with love and the wondrous ability to see it in all living creatures. Their sweetness and love of God will live forever in my poems.

The second two are my beautiful daughters, Julie and Stacey, both endowed with loving hearts and a wonderful sense of humor. Without their caring and support this book would have never been written and my life would truly have no meaning. I love you all with all my heart. Thank you.

Preface

The writings of these poems are the result, as well as the cure, of personal hardships experienced throughout the life of the author. It gives hope to all, that from the ashes of death, divorce and pain, we can all rise again to meet an even greater challenge, the continuance of our own lives. And that even in the darkest times of loneliness and fear, a little flicker of hope burns brightly in our souls. This little flame, combined with love and a never ending faith in God, can take us all on a wonderful journey down the path of life, sensing all the beauty and goodness it truly beholds.

These poems are not contrivances or adaptations, they are the heart and soul of the author. They are his life. Written with the hope that everyone will find something in his poems to lift their spirits and remember, once again, that you truly never walk alone.

ACKNOWLEDGMENTS

Stacey Hoey Burns
Daughter, friend and constant supporter of my dream

Julie Hoey McHugh
Daughter, friend and eternal cheerleader

Mary Roberts
Dearest friend and mentor, whose dedication to my dream
was endless

Laura Reeve
My guardian angel and sympathetic ear

I love and thank you all!

Poem of Introduction

This poem of introduction
    Simply tells the reason why
I've written all the poems inside
    To lift our spirits high

For these are merely stories
    Of all the things I've seen
I've suffered through divorce and death
    And know what loss can mean

I almost died of heart disease
    In nineteen-eighty-two
And know what fear is all about
    I've lived it just like you

But now my life has meaning
    For I've found a dearest friend
He walks with me on beaches
    And He lets me live again

You'll see Him in my poetry
    And sense Him in the rhyme
He's there for me in smiles or tears
    He's with me all the time

So if you choose to read my poems
    And I truly hope you do
Share with me the light of hope
    That's there for me and you

Snowfall

Of all the things in life I've seen
    Throughout these precious years
Snowfalls capture all my thoughts
    And wash away my fears

They're quiet, soft, when wisping down
    To cover what we see
It takes the very worst of things
    And powders them for me

It always seems so still at night
    When first it has arrived
It takes the dried out winter tree
    And makes it come alive

It covers all the shrubs and leaves
    That stay throughout the year
And makes it all look beautiful
    So fresh and white and clear

It covers all the ugly things
    That we would always see
And creates another masterpiece
    That's painted just for me

It never stops to pick and choose
    Which item it should bless
It just drifts down on everything
    And makes it look its best

Oh wouldn't it be wonderful
    If life had snowfalls, too
That came into our hearts and minds
    And made them all brand new

That covered all the evil thoughts
   And whitened all the pain
And every time we're sad or low
   It would simply snow again

So this I pray for everyone
   That feels a little blue
That snow will drift into your heart
   And make it fresh and new

That all the dark and worrisome thoughts
   You think of every night
Will be snowed upon with happy thoughts
   That cover all your frights

For all the beauty life beholds
   Is like a snowfall, too
It puts aside the ugliness
   And covers it for you

Just let it snow into your heart
   And always in your mind
And keep them fresh and clean my friend
   Pure thoughts are the only kind

So every time you see it snow
   And it happens every year
You'll know you're growing older
   And there's less and less to fear

Because it's snowing harder now
   And life is clear and bright
And in these last snowfalls of life
   Your hair is turning white

The Wind and I

I think I've spent most all of my life
    Simply trying to catch the wind
To hold the power within my hands
    And feel its strength within

It's so illusive this billowy friend
    That I never seem to find
It's like the happiness I've often sought
    That hides somewhere in my mind

I know it's out there, I've seen it work
    On waves and trees and flowers
I've seen it take a kite up high
    And hold it there for hours

But it never fails to stop again
    Just when I'm ready to fly
Like lovers, friends and relationships
    That all of a sudden die

So why can't the wind stay longer true
    And keep that kite in the air
And why can't love stay longer too
    That seems only more than fair

But I guess the answer is in God's hands
    He knows when to stop and end
And I'll simply have to wait and see
    Just how the wind will bend

Some days it's scary like a hurricane
    That screams all day and night
Other days calm and almost serene
    Like watching a gull in flight

It turns and puffs and gales and roars
    Like the way our life takes form
But stops again on a beautiful note
    That's the calm right after the storm

So I guess I'll take this wonderful ride
    Just my friend the wind and me
And see where it takes me in my life
    Like the leaf that falls from the tree

I only hope that where I land
    I will simply and finally find
That wonderful life and sweetest love
    That's been forever on my mind

For I know she's out there flying around
    With all the twists and turns
Looking for me and a place to land
    In my heart where the love light burns

So listen to me now old friend
    And know what I'm saying is true
You've blown so hard and so very long
    That by now you should be through

It's time for calm and serenity
    It's time for you to cower
Just like it's time for me to slow
    And stop to smell the flowers

So let's work together one more time
    And bring me peace from above
I've seen the storms and the hurricanes
    It's time for the morning of love

Little Bird

Fly away little bird
 Soar in azure sky
Heart of mighty titans
 Never fear to die

Untethered flight of freedom
 Brave heart sweetly soars
Visualizing all creation
 As he flies the sun drenched shore

Fly away little bird
 Let us know your heart
Tell us what it's like to feel
 Such freedom from the start

True example exultation
 Pure joy in God's design
O that we exemplify
 Your kind and loving mind

Sing your song in trills of love
 That kiss our mortal ear
Your melody of Godliness
 So sweet and void of fear

Fly away little bird
 Hold me in your sight
Stay close in fading sunset
 For I'll lose you in the night

Hear My Love

Please listen to my love
   Be close and hear
Your face is held within my hands
   I'll whisper in your ear

I'll speak of love
   It's here, it's now
The voice you hear is from the heart
   It tells the love I vow

Please listen to my love
   Know how much I care
Feel how much you mean to me
   Know I'm always there

Put your head upon my chest
   Hear my warmth of heart
Keep me close within your dreams
   As one and not apart

Please listen to my love
   It's here right now, it's near
Maybe only for today
   Perhaps a life of years

Whispers of I love you
   Touch that means the same
Please listen to my love
   It may never come again

I Met A Man

I met a man while walking
   His clothes were ripped and torn
I ask him if he needed help
   He laughed at me in scorn

And then he smiled with blackened teeth
   And coughed into his sleeve
He said that I should know him well
   And turned to take his leave

I quickly grabbed him by the coat
   And turned him fast around
And saw the old man cower in fear
   As tears came streaming down

He softly spoke, much kinder now
   In a voice I thought I knew
And told me he was simply me
   And my vision saw it, too

He said that this would be my life
   If I didn't change my ways
Stop fretting what the future holds
   Start living for today

Don't shudder at commitment
   And learn to love again
Forget the pain and heartache past
   And let the memory end

You've done the best that you can do
    You've given all you can
So try to build your life anew
    It's time that you began

So stand erect and take the walk
    Be proud of what you are
A kind and gentle, loving man
    With the mind to take you far

For the future doesn't need to be
    This man before your eyes
Simply trust in the Father, and open your heart
    And you're in for a pleasant surprise

So pray every night and wake up ever day
    Feeling thankful and happy to be
And please don't forget how to love once again
    Or you'll end in the gutter like me

Still Pond

Deep inside the densest woods
    A still pond lies at rest
A mirrored glass reflecting pool
    Serenity at best

A quiet place that imitates
    The beauty all around
And simply lies in tranquil state
    Just waiting to be found

For beauty must be witnessed
    To earn its proper place
Like ocean waves that pound the shores
    Or a smile on a beautiful face

But if you discover a still pond
    Take the time to absorb what it means
A place undefiled by the scourges of man
    Where you quietly conjure your dreams

Where dragonflies play in the sunshine
    And butterflies light on the tree
A place where your heart can be peaceful
    And the Father can whisper to thee

For this is creation, perfection, and love
    It's His lesson in peace just for you
Remember to thank Him and follow His lead
    Be a still pond in all that you do

A Little Bit

A little bit is good sometimes
   A little bit of that
I think I'll only have a little
   So I won't get really fat

I'll see you in a little while
   Please tell me what that means
We say that they have little ones
   That's children so it seems

We're having a little problem
   Now this one's really good
For these are always really bad
   I wish I understood

Little by little we meet in the middle
   Is one I'll never see
If we meet in the middle just where did we start
   And where does that put me

Give a little take a little
   This one seems really fair
'Cause if we only give and take
   We'll still have more to share

Yes little things still mean a lot
   And little words are sweet
So give a little, love a little
   These little things repeat

They say let's make a little love
   Now this one makes me smile
'Cause a little always means a lot
   And takes more than a little while

From the Ashes

Fire the great destroyer
   Of everything it sees
The heartless, mindless carnivore
   That blackens as it feeds

Reducing all the beauty
   To ashes pale and gray
Reminders of the things we loved
   It quickly stole away

For death, divorce and hurt and pain
   Are fire like in their own
They take away the ones you love
   And ruin many homes

They turn the bluest day to gray
   And burn the kindest heart
Turn promises to emptiness
   And rip your world apart

Yet somewhere in the ashes
   When you've lost the will to cope
The smallest ember flickers bright
   This little spark of hope

For hope is really all we have
   And love is what we need
To rise again from ashes gray
   And once again succeed

To lead a life of happiness
   And practice how to smile
Forget the fear of finding love
   It's been there all the while

Simply learn to live again
   And savor every day
We only have the time that's left
   Start living for today

Love Letters

While sifting through the attic
    In the place where memories graze
I came across a dusty box
    Tightly nestled in the maze

Though truly nondescriptive
    I could sense it wasn't mine
And it cast a look of stay away
    As I gently cut the twine

Inside I found the letters
    That my father sent from sea
Five years he served upon these ships
    In a war so far from me

My parents both have passed away
    Yet it's wonderful to see
The kind of love and dreams they had
    For the future that would be

And though my mom was all alone
    With a child and a husband at sea
She'd always reread all the letters he sent
    And would smile as the tears trickled free

Yet today as I sit here with letters in hand
    I feel sad the love letter's passé
For long distance and faxes and E-mail and such
    Have all taken the romance away

So now in my fifties, I've taken a stand
  To write letters to one that I care
And even though sent to a neighboring town
  It's romantic and ever so rare

So in years quickly faded and time that's elapsed
  With our children all married and grown
They can climb to the attic, where memories are kept
  Just ponder the past, on their own

But stuffed in the corner, in a box wrapped in twine
  And all covered in dust of the years
They'll find letters of love, that I wrote to their mom
  Slightly stained with the smiles and tears

A Walk With Thee

Sometimes I walk along the beach
   And know I'm not alone
I know I've been here many times
   But still I'm coming home

I feel a presence by my side
   That warms my heart with love
There's no one else, it's only me
   And my friend that dwells above

For God is with me every day
   I know He's always there
I feel Him in the warmth of sun
   And slightest puffs of air

I see Him in the gull in flight
   And hear Him in the waves
And know He's always there for me
   Like the other souls He saves

For God lives truly in my heart
   And always in my mind
He teaches me to love and share
   The beauty that I find

He helps me when I write my poems
   Of love and hurt and pain
And helps me when I need to know
   That love will come again

For something sweet has happened now
 A calming so it seems
I feel that writing gives me strength
 And lets me live my dreams

For poetry is truly love
 It's written from the heart
It's given out to those who share
 This loving form of art

And every day I'm thankful
 As I walk along the sand
And know I'll never be alone
 As He always holds my hand

For life for me is calmer now
 And days are ever sweet
So take the time to walk my walk
 And pray you two will meet

Remember Me

As I approach seniority
   My mind is cluttered thought
Of how I would remember me
   Lest my life would be for naught

I always tried to do my best
   Yet failed on several tries
But a man who never takes a chance
   Seldom yields to feeling alive

For life is opportunity
   To search and try to find
The reason God created me
   With a gentle loving mind

For the title of my life is love
   And caring is the theme
And I've finally found the confidence
   To write the things I dream

So if I haven't garnered wealth
   Before He calls me home
Please don't feel I've wasted
   All the hours I've spent alone

For my poetry has brought me hope
   And expresses how I feel
It's eased the pain and sorrows
   That for me were ever real

It also speaks of promise
And the wonder life beholds
And to love each precious moment
As this wondrous tale unfolds

It speaks of love of family
And always holds them near
For my daughters truly are my love
And the reason that I'm here

To watch them grow and share their lives
With men I'm proud to know
And their children that reflect the love
They forever seem to show

For grandkids are another chance
To teach what love can be
And life is always sweeter
When you have one on your knee

Now I hope I'll be around awhile
As my life begins anew
And be with someone dear to me
As we share the things we do

But no matter what the future holds
And no matter where I'll be
You'll always have my poetry
Words of love, to you, from me

There's a Quiet Place

There's a quiet place within my heart,
    a place where love grows without fear,
    that knows only soft words and whispers
There's little light that softly burns
    and sweetly fires the thoughts of love to be
    and ignites the inspirations of the loving heart
There's a quiet place within my soul
    where God can feed my loneliness with hope
    and lead me forth to love again another day
There's a peaceful time at sunrise
    where my thoughts reflect on painful yesterdays
    and give thanks for the promise of tomorrow
There's a quiet place within my heart
    where the seed of love has begun to blossom
    into a never ending story, called you and I

Fly My Sparrow

Fly my sparrow
   Elevate the heart
Show us exultation
   If only to depart

Be the winds avenger
   Soar with eagle pride
Rocket to the mountain
   With gravity defied

Unleash the bridled power
   Slice through azure sky
With heart so quickly pounding
   No fear of when to die

Dive upon the beaches
   Storm the greenest woods
Tell me what it's like to fly
   If only that I could

Remind me how it feels to soar
   So void of fear and pain
Fly with me beneath your wing
   Through sun and darkest rain

For I so like the sparrow sweet
   Should fly ever fearless and free
For the beauty of life passes by ever swift
   In the flight God created for me

Sunset Bay

Some evenings close to sunset
   I walk out to the bay
And find a cozy place to sit
   And watch the end of day

For lurking in the western sky
   The ball of fire descends
Creating God's own masterpiece
   That thrills me once again

For as it drops to kiss the earth
   The painting comes alive
And clouds explode in wondrous hues
   That dance before my eyes

With the beauty of the rainbow
   Only splashed across the west
I sense the beauty life beholds
   With warmth upon my chest

And as the birds decease to sing
   And winds are frozen still
The bay will turn to mirrored glass
   And duplicate His will

Yet as the cloak of evening falls
   To blacken all I see
I take the time to thank the Lord
   For all His gifts to me

For sunsets come and go my friend
   Like the tide that embraces the shore
Take time to enjoy them and always give thanks
   For someday they'll be gone evermore

My Star

I believe that everyone
  Has been assigned a star
And though a million miles away
  It knows right where you are

It twinkles brightly every day
  And even through the night
It shows us all the way to go
  In the journey we call life

And though it isn't visible
  When clouds and storms appear
It's always up there blinking
  Every moment of the year

And I know that there are millions
  Scattered all across the sky
And they represent each one of us
  Still blinking 'til we die

And every night I watch them
  Many new ones will appear
They're all the new-born babies
  With the little blinks so dear

And some nights when you look above
  And a few of them are gone
Know quite well they've passed away
  And will soon be coming home

For stars reside in heaven
    Kind of landing lights, you see
And they indicate direction
    To the place we want to be

For God created all the earth
    And all the heavens too
So find your star and watch it close
    As He placed it there for you

And if you ever feel alone
    Just simply look above
It blinks for you and no one else
    It's the signal of His love

So never fear and walk the path
    That always takes you home
For God is with you, hand in hand
    And He never will leave you alone

Fog

Some mornings when I rise to see
   The sun exploding east
I look outside and realize
   I've been shrouded by the beast

Its cloak has fallen all around
   And draped my world in gray
And stolen all the colors
   From my new and glorious day

The sky and clouds have disappeared
   Just like the dunes and sea
And I can only hear the roar
   Two-hundred feet from me

And everything is wet outside
   From this quiet sulking mist
It's taken all the flowers and trees
   And closed them in its fist

For fog is like a temptress
   And sometimes pulls away
To give a glimpse of what it hides
   Your bright and sunny day

But never fear for very soon
   The wind will rise up strong
And push the fog back out to sea
   To the place where it belongs

Yet the nicest thing about the fog
   As it moves away from shore
You'll be thankful for this lovely day
   And appreciate it more

Sisters

Sisters always puzzle me
    They're hard to understand
They love each other very much
    But seldom show their hand

They don't keep contact all the time
    Yet each one seems to know
The time to phone or write the note
    When the other's feeling low

Their memories are amazing
    Of their times together past
Old boy friends, school and sister stuff
    That can always make them laugh

They also know they have a place
    To reveal their love and pain
And know that once the story's told
    It will never repeat again

So having a sister's like having a shrink
    Who charges you one twenty-five
But this one is free, knows you better than most
    And will see you whenever you try

So if you marry a sister, as men often do
    And you think that you'll come in between
Don't be foolish my friend, for she'll pack up again
    And move back to her sister in Queens

Morning

Morning's always my favorite time
   It feels so good to me
To wake up early every day
   And see the sun break free

To hear the birds awake to chime
   And hear the wind begin
To know that God has given me
   Another gift from Him

Every morning seems to me
   Like another chance to grow
A new beginning, a brand new start
   Not knowing where it will go

It's fresh and clean as fallen snow
   And was never here before
Like newborn babies, budding flowers
   And fresh sand along the shore

I have another chance in life
   To make the wrong things right
To try to love and care for those
   Who cannot see the light

To give more of myself today
   As much as I may dare
To show the people close to me
   How much I really care

This is my time, this day's for me
   To do whatever I choose
So I guess I better do my best
   Or one more chance I'll lose

To make a difference in someone's life
    No matter how great or small
For isn't that what life's about
    Helping others after all

So this I vow to you my friend
    No matter who you may be
To make the best of this beautiful day
    In hopes that you may see

The gift that He has given us
    And what it means to love
These beautiful mornings on this earth
    That come from up above

We're only here a little while
    We're simply passing through
So look around and take it in
    This gift He gives to you

Don't waste your time with worrisome thoughts
    And always try to smile
Before you know it this day's lost
    It's only here for awhile

This is your moment, this is your time
    It all belongs to you
So take it now and hold it close
    For this I know is true

We only have just once around
    One time to do it right
So love and help someone else today
    For soon it will be night

The Dentist

Whenever it's time for me to list
    The things I truly fear
The dentist wins it all hands down
    It's the one I won't go near

For ever since my childhood days
    When I climbed up in the chair
And the needle hit my gums so hard
    That it nearly curled my hair

And then he smiled, that sleezy smile
    And told me he'd be back
And my face would turn to rubber
    When he came for the second attack

And then, oh boy, it finally came
    The drill that was screaming and loud
As it entered my tooth it went into the nerve
    And I thought I would jump to the clouds

Now I know that I sound like a sissy to you
    But we're talking some horrible pain
And after he probed and he pushed for awhile
    He came back and he did it again

And now that I'm sweating and shaking inside
    And my nerves are all tingly and cold
He asked me to spit it right into the bowl
    With the lips that my teeth couldn't hold

So you slobber and dribble and feel like a fool
    And you talk with a tongue that is lead
As you try to explain in the language of mush
    That the side of your eye just went dead

But at last it's the time, when there's really no pain
    When he fills it and levels it down
And I rinse and I spit and I finally breathe
    Yet my face hasn't yet come around

And as I walk home, and I light up a smoke
    And the cigarette falls on the floor
I promise myself, that I'll brush every day
    And I'll never return anymore

And so now today, when appointments are set
    And I enter the room with the chair
I request to be shot with the sodium pen
    And I never will know I was there

The Only Child

The only child is a lonely child
    And goes through life that way
No brothers or sisters to reflect upon
    Just he alone every day

He makes his own decisions
    For he's the only one
To say what's right or maybe wrong
    This path is his alone

When I was young and growing up
    People would always say
He must be spoiled, he gets it all
    But what about today

It's only me who takes the time
    To pat me on the back
To tell myself I'm doing fine
    And it's okay to look back

People never understand
    What it's like to be alone
No brothers, sisters, husbands or wives
    No one to call your own

If it wasn't for my daughters
    Whose support has been so strong
They're always there as my best friends
    As I go stumbling on

It's taken time for me to grasp
　　This idea it's only me
Who can make me smile or even laugh
　　But that's okay you see

Because I have to answer
　　Eventually it seems
Only to myself and God
　　The partner in my dreams

He knows me well and keeps me straight
　　Down life's ever winding path
And with Him always by my side
　　It's easier to laugh

To know that there will come a day
　　Of this I'm truly sure
When life again will smile on me
　　And I'll feel much more secure

It's time for me to move along
　　And face whatever comes
For I must do it by myself
　　For it's my true one song

To be the best that I can be
　　And show the world it's true
That the only people in this world
　　Can be happy just like you

Tinsel

Tinsel came into this world
    Far back as I can see
It always hung below the boughs
    Of all our Christmas trees

The first I saw was heavy
    Kind of lead-like, hanging down
But later came the lighter stuff
    So sleek and wisping 'round

It was the final crowning touch
    Came just before the end
And everyone was there to help
    Their talents for to lend

It truly was good therapy
    A family working as one
And every one of us was pleased
    When the job was finally done

But Christmas time was over
    And the old tree would come down
And one thing you could bet for sure
    There was tinsel all around

You'd find it stuck into the rug
    On sofas, tables and chairs
And even after you were through
    You'd find it in your hair

But finally the tree was gone
   And sat outside the gate
Just waiting for that city truck
   To take it to its fate

It was sad to see it waiting
   Sitting out there in the cold
Kind of lonely, as some folks I know
   When they were getting old

Yet every spring when I go out
   And walk on new grown grass
I see it hanging on a bush
   For it will always last

It's telling us that Christmas
   Will be with us all year long
And those who would think otherwise
   My friend, are very wrong

For Christmas is the season
   To be thankful for His birth
That He alone forgave our sins
   And blessed us on this earth

So if you're not using tinsel
   I suggest you better start
And remember Christmas all year long
   And keep Christ in your heart

The Bag Pipes

I hear the pipes at sundown
   As I'm walking on the sand
The man is probably seventy-five
   With large and gnarled hands

He's tall and always walks with pride
   With a slowness to his stride
He's tan and wears the whitest shirt
   And a kilt of green beside

His music truly haunts the air
   It's eerie, but it's sweet
It seems to take you back in time
   Old songs that still repeat

The pipes just sound so heavenly
   It's God's instrument I'm sure
It plays the strains of love and death
   That always sound so pure

It congers up a distant land
   That's somehow in the past
And reaches deep within my soul
   As the sun is sinking fast

So if you ever see the piper
   Walking evenings on the sand
Know that God is listening, too
   As He walks you hand in hand

A Kinder Place

I've been looking for a kinder place
    where people speak in gentle voices,
    and anger and hate have been extinguished

I've been looking for a kinder place
    where friendships grow as swift as flowers,
    and children play freely without fear

I've been looking for a kinder place
    where goodness and caring are the measure,
    and leaders are the kindest and most giving

I've been looking for a kinder place
    where walking with God
    is truly not the road less traveled

Today I found a kinder place
    and realized I've been there all along,
    for it lies sweetly within my heart and soul

Has Anyone Seen My Little Girls

Has anyone seen my little girls
   The ones I used to hold
And rock to sleep with lullabies
   Of wonders to behold

Has anyone seen my little girls
   I used to walk to school
The ones with silky golden hair
   I taught to hustle pool

Has anyone seen my little girls
   Who used to fight with boys
The terrors of the soccer field
   With true athletic poise

Has anyone seen my little girls
   Who frolicked in the waves
And filled my life with warmth and joy
   Like sunny summer days

Has anyone seen my little girls
   I held to quiet tears
And loved with all my heart and soul
   And shared the best of years

Has anyone seen my little girls
   Their women now you see
Both beautiful and talented
   The proudest part of me

And both have men that love them dear
  And one with children three
And each has found their strength in God
  And care for all that be

Has anyone seen my little girls
  Is just a poem of pride
To show my daughters how much love
  Their father holds inside

He's Here

Some people always look for God
   They peer into the sky
They hunger for His presence
   In this world of you and I

And I always find it humorous
   That they never look around
And see the beauty life beholds
   The place He's always found

He's always living in your heart
   And ever in your mind
For all the loving things you do
   Are from His own design

I see Him in the mountains high
   And waves that kiss the sand
I sense Him in the eagle's flight
   And fields that blanket land

I sense Him in the tallest trees
   And birds that sweetly sing
For all the wondrous things in life
   Are simply gifts He brings

For God created everything
   And did it all with care
To show you all the love He has
   And what it means to share

And as I write these words, I stop
  And slowly start to smile
For all the folks that look for God
  Have been with Him awhile

For if you truly do believe
  Your search may be in vain
Simply look inside your heart
  You'll find Him once again

He's always there, He never left
  It's only you that's blind
Open up your heart and soul
  His presence there to find

So walk with Him and talk with Him
  And know your loving friend
He's been beside you all your life
  And will hold you in the end

The First Snow

On an evening in December
   When the temperatures are low
You look above and see the moon
   That's ringed with signs of snow

And then you sense it in the air
   That old familiar feel
And weathermen have all agreed
   The possibility's real

You crawl into the quilted warmth
   And wonder what will be
When first you rise tomorrow morn
   And what your eyes will see

And then you rise at break of dawn
   And scramble out of bed
And toddle to the window first
   For proof of what they said

And there, before your morning eyes
   The world is new and bright
And everything that once was brown
   Has donned a cloak of white

And though you've seen it many times
   The first is always best
And when you dress and walk outside
   You feel it in your chest

The crispness and the purity
    Of air that follows snow
The freshest breath a soul can take
    As cheeks begin to glow

For as in life and snowfalls too
    Sometimes the first is best
First car, first date, first kiss, first love
    The rest seem something less

But always know within your heart
    Though times are filled with pain
That snow and love will come again
    And cover what was stained

For only God creates the firsts
    Whether snowfalls or kisses or love
But never lose hope, if you've failed in the first
    He has seconds and thirds up above

Stay in Kindergarten

Always stay in kindergarten
   Follow all the rules
Never try to graduate
   And act like other fools

Learn the basic lessons well
   And keep them close to heart
Strive for pure simplicity
   Keep right and wrong apart

And always treat your classmates well
   Be gentle, kind, and sweet
And always speak when spoken to
   And smile at those you meet

Only take what's rightly yours
   And always try to share
Help the others on their way
   And take the time to care

Never curse or raise your voice
   And learn to get along
And never cease to bow your head
   And pray with heart so strong

And if you truly practice well
   As little children do
You may find life a sweeter place
   And sense a nicer you

For all the things you truly need
    To face each trying day
Were put into your mind at five
    And just a thought away

So never fear to wander back
    And gather what you know
Repeat the kindergarten class
    And watch your knowledge grow

And always pledge to recognize
    How basic life can be
For faith and honor, truth and love
    Build a character in thee

So when you're sitting at your desk
    And bow your head in prayer
Take the time to thank the Lord
    Your childhood's always there

I'm So Tired

I'm so tired
   For sleep escapes me now
Worry's her replacement
   Depression takes a bow

Weary true description
   Inability to fight
Surrender calls me softly
   In the darkest throes of night

Reason for existence
   Smothered in the pain
Sadness inescapable
   So frightening to remain

Always praying fervently
   Searching for the end
When confidence and happiness
   Will surface once again

Tired of self made loneliness
   Exhausted from my fears
Robbed of all commitment
   Always threatened by my years

Only God in all His wisdom
   Can save this mortal soul
I beseech Him every waking day
   To guide me in my role

He's held me in my darkest hours
Through death, divorce and pain
Instilled in me eternal hope
That life will smile again

For hope is truly all we have
It's the blessing that He gives
And hopelessness can blind the faith
And cease the will to live

So I'll continue hoping
And I'll pray for the strength to succeed
With God as my partner, turn darkness to light
Find the peace that I desperately need

The Dreamer

The dreamer is a lonely man
   With dreams forever real
He looks at life in a promising way
   That you may never feel

He believes in love and all the things
   He imagines to be true
And feels that life holds all things dear
   Like the love he has for you

He never doubts his feelings
   That come from deep within
He knows these are the sweetest songs
   To be sung by only him

For it's his life and canvas
   That only he can paint
And only he creates the strokes
   Either powerful or faint

He can tell you what he wants from life
   His beautiful design
For it's always in his heart and soul
   And forever on his mind

He knows it should be quiet and sweet
   Passing gently every day
Be full of love and tenderness
   As the seasons float away

For dreamers really are the source
    For what we want to hear
That life gets better every day
    And will throughout the year

That there's beauty in the future
    And promise in every smile
So grab each one and hold it close
    It only lasts awhile

That time can be your greatest friend
    If you only use it well
Don't waste the seconds feeling down
    Or waiting for the bell

For it's your round and it's your time
    To dream what's good for you
So go for all the dreams you wish
    And even add a few

I dream of things I haven't seen
    Or loved until today
But this one's new and fresh to me
    It's mine to dream away

I know I have the power
    And truly have the soul
To love again another time
    Before my bell will toll

So see each day with promise
    Another wonderful chance
To start again and smile again
    To love, to sing and dance

To wander in the warmth of life
   To dream what it may hold
Don't be afraid to make the moves
   That some consider bold

This is the only dream you have
   Your one day in the sun
So imagine all the things you want
   And fill your days with fun

So just be the dreamer and never by shy
   To dream for only you
For some of us truly know all too well
   There are dreams that can really come true

I Just Don't Fit

Sometimes I stand and look at life
    And know I just don't fit
An oddity of sorts I am
    Who stands when others sit

I look at life so differently
    Unlike the folks I know
Who walk the path with blinders on
    And never see the show

They strive to reach for great success
    Yet never know the why
They value all commodities
    And miss the morning sky

But as for me, I look at life
    As precious and divine
And pleased that God has given me
    This wondrous gift of time

Time to share and time to love
    The sweetest gift of all
For some folks walk the path alone
    And never chance to fall

I take the time to walk the beach
    And trod the woods and streams
To sense creation in my heart
    And never cease to dream

For life is fleeting by each day
    And suns will rise and fall
And moons will light the evening sky
    In wonder to us all

So if you live your life at speed
    To garner wealth and fame
Remember all the wasted years
    You've lost to play the game

It doesn't matter who you are
    Or even what you own
For everything will simply stop
    When the Father calls you home

So though you think I may be strange
    And even wasting time
Just think of all the things you'll miss
    While fighting for the dime

For if my time would come today
    I know one thing is true
I've tasted life at every turn
    And loved with passion too

So take the time my pressured friend
    To stop and sense the day
It happens just once, and it never returns
    This is life that you're wasting away

The Funeral

Eve of wrenching sadness
   Room of endless tears
Memories awash in pain
   Recalling yesteryears

Families huddled closely
   Flowers sickening sweet
Casket bright and polished
   Friends lined in sobbing seats

The ever painful greetings
   Hugs and handshakes, too
Kisses on the cheek that say
   We're always here for you

Prayers forever flowing
   Time that seems to crawl
The minister with words of love
   For the heart that touched us all

And slowly, ever slowly
   The friends begin to leave
And suddenly you're all alone
   The family left to grieve

With streaming tears and sad good-bys
   And hearts that ache with pain
You're led away to solitude
   Where you gather composure again

But one person missed as they counted the roll
   Of the friends ever caring and grand
Was the vision of God, ever loving and kind
   As He left with your friend hand in hand

I've Got a Little Secret

I've got a little secret
   That I keep within my heart
A friend that always walks with me
   And loved me from the start

He's always there to give me strength
   In times of hurt and pain
And fills my heart with love and joy
   And lets me smile again

He walks with me along the beach
   And holds his hand in mine
And teaches me to love my life
   And care for all I find

He stood beside me through it all
   Through death, divorce and pain
And led me down the path of hope
   And let me live again

I'm sure you understand by now
   That God's my dearest friend
And though I walk alone in life
   He's with me 'til the end

I've got a little secret
   And I'll share it with you, too
Take the time to walk with God
   And you'll savor the wonder of you

Little Children

The joy of little children
  Little giggles full of love
Simply awed with all the wonder
  With the gifts from God above

Always splashing in the puddles
  Ever digging in the sand
Creativity with mud pies
  And forever washing hands

In motion never ceasing
  Always first to question why
They need to know the answers
  And won't stop until you try

They love to cuddle close beside
  When sitting on the couch
And listen to the story read
  That they memorized throughout

They're picky little eaters
  Only tasting what they know
And get really kind of itchy
  If the time is passing slow

Then when excused they rocket by
  And return to fun and games
And will run 'til sheer exhaustion
  Calls the time for bed again

And after bath and brushing teeth
　　You can slowly watch them fade
And with only half a story told
　　They fall victim to sleep that they crave

For the sleeping child is a beautiful sight
　　So content with the power to dream
Yet in only eight hours he's back in the race
　　Full of energy, questions and screams

Sleep well mom and dad

Old Sneakers

I have these beat up sneakers
    That I wear most every day
They're scuffed and kind of shapeless
    Truly should be thrown away

But I've not the heart to tell them
    That the end if finally here
For they've been with me so very long
    Much like friends I hold so dear

We've been through mud and rain and snow
    And walked the miles of sand
And even though they're looking tired
    They can dance to beat the band

I know I must replace my friends
    With sneakers fresh and white
But I've always had the hardest time
    Doing something that doesn't seem right

For if friends appear a little tired
    And maybe even sad
You simply can't just walk away
    And replace the ones you had

So I'll keep them in the closet
    Just like friends you hold in heart
And though they're not with me today
    We're never truly apart

For the rainy days will come again
    And the new ones fear the trial
So I'll reach back for the ones I trust
    Who have partnered my stormiest miles

And always remember old sneakers and friends
    Are a lot like each other you see
If I reach in the closet or deep in my heart
    I'll find love always waiting for me

The Puppet

The puppet is a little doll
    Who's often made of wood
Controlled by strings in someone's hand
    That's surely understood

And we control the moves he makes
    And the way that he reacts
We make him sit or stand or walk
    Give him movement that he lacks

We can make him raise his arms up high
    We can even make him smile
For the puppet does our bidding well
    Simply aping all the while

Yet it seems to me some people act
    The way some puppets do
They watch how others live their lives
    And imitate them too

They're always acting out a part
    That was written for someone else
Instead of loving who they are
    And the pleasure of being yourself

So remove all the strings, learn to march on your own
    For your drummer is always at hand
It's your time and your life, simply live it your way
    And you'll be a much happier man

Time

Time has always seemed to me
    The greatest gift of all
For only God can grant the days
    Until our final call

For each of us is given time
    Never knowing where it ends
We only have just once around
    That's the message that He sends

There's time to smile and time to care
    To laugh, to sing, and cry
But most of all there's time for us
    To love until we die

So take the time to help someone
    Less fortunate than you
For your life will be remembered
    By the loving acts you do

And always try to make the time
    For your loved ones and your friends
For this is time that's wisely spent
    And will never come again

And always try to live your life
    Like you have so little time
Don't wait to see the friend who's ill
    Or the loved ones on your mind

And always say the things you feel
   To those you hold so dear
For time is not a guarantee
   Of days or months or years

And always take the time to pray
   To thank Him for the time
He's given just to you alone
   To cherish and to find

The ways in life to fill your time
   With happiness and love
Because the clock runs fast my friend
   And it's only wound above

Thanksgiving

It happens each November
   And it never fails to show
It's the time we call Thanksgiving
   When the warmest feelings flow

It's families all together
   And friends that gather near
Giving thanks for what they've had
   Throughout the previous year

There're turkeys, hams and corn and squash
   As well as candied yams
And apple, minced and pumpkin pies
   All made by mothers hand

And we gather round the table
   Giving thanks to God above
For all the things He's brought to us
   Like this meal prepared with love

For giving thanks should never be
   A seasonal event
Be thankful to Him every day
   For the blessings that He sent

And fill your life with love and care
   And always keep Him near
And simply be thankful for all that you have
   'Til you gather together next year

Antiques

Antiques are found most everywhere
    In garages, homes and stores
They're wondrous recollections
    Of a time that passed before

They take us back into the past
    And tweak our memory, too
And always seem more eloquent
    Than the things we find brand new

They're furniture and crystal lamps
    Old books and hand blown glass
They're comic books and cars and games
    All the beauty of the past

But the ones I truly find most loved
    Are seventy years or more
They're usually found in nursing homes
    Or reside in the house next door

They're the senior citizens in this world
    The ones He has chosen to stay
To reflect on the past and a glorious time
    Much more simple and pure than today

For they have the knowledge and used all the things
    That we feel are incredible finds
They were glasses and chairs that they used every day
    Never giving it really much mind

So if you crave the knowledge of things from the past
    Simply find one and go for a walk
For these are the only antiques that I know
    That hold hands and can actually talk

The Sweet Winds Blow

(by the author at age 14)

The wind blows fast across the sea
    It blows from distant lands to me
It told of terror, worry and fear
    Yet it was just the wind upon my ear

The sky was dark, the moon not seen
    But still the fear was there it seemed
O why must there be winds or fear
    Instead of sweet winds on my ear

The wind still blows upon my ear
    Yet somehow I have lost the fear
The fear winds nor more come to me
    Because dear friend I'm deaf you see
        1956

Good-bye to Love

To say good-bye to one you love
   Inflicts the worst of pain
The erasure of the memories
   That will never come again

You gave your heart and all your soul
   To one who couldn't learn
Acceptance of the love you gave
   Or to love you in return

But fault is not important here
   And blame is not the theme
The only thing that matters now
   Is the dying of the dream

The promise of the future
   Is over for today
Until I fall in love again
   And give my heart away

For the nicest things about the heart
   Is how it knows to mend
And stands behind you when it's time
   To fall in love again

For maybe this time, maybe next
   That someone will be there
Who truly knows what loving is
   And what it means to share

I know this lady does exist
   God's holding her you see
I'm ready now to share my life
   Please release her love to me

There Will Come A Day I Pray

There will come a day, I pray
   When peace will rule the world
And all the battle flags of war
   Will stand there sweetly furled

There will come a day I pray
   When love will be the creed
And all the money spent on war
   Will help the ones in need

There will come a day I pray
   When children everywhere
Will have the food they need to eat
   And lots of love and care

There will come a day I pray
   When you and I agree
Until then, I'll pray for you
   And hope you'll pray for me

Free To Be Me

I'm free to be me
    The who that I am
Possibilities endless
    The best that I can

To be quietly calm
    Or scream at the night
To wander on beaches
    And sense with delight

To taste all the sweetness
    Of life passing by
And garner the beauty
    That passes the eye

For it's my decision
    To be all that I may
To rise and enjoy
    This miraculous day

For life can be painful
    And scary at best
But I know I can win
    When I'm put to the test

For I have a secret
    I keep in my heart
The love of the Father
    Who never departs

He walks close beside me
   And shows me the way
To love all the wonders
   I see every day

He holds me in sadness
   And smiles when I laugh
And teaches forgiveness
   For sins of the past

So I'll keep on praying
   And smiling so free
For with God as my mentor
   I'm the best I can be

Tired of Everything

I'm so tired of all the pressures that
   life can deal
Tired of all the success bound cannibals,
   always ready to pounce at my slightest mistake
Tired of those who smile for what you have,
   and never sensing what you truly are
I'm tired of those so void of dreams, and
   trapped in their own egotistic party game
Tired of endless threats from those who
   would take everything you own for small reward
And tired beyond all time of failing to be
   myself, and apologizing for the man I
   truly am.
A sensitive and quiet man, that's full of love
   and cares deeply for those who love him in return
Who simply wants to walk the earth in peace
   and savor all the wonders life beholds
A man that only wants to follow the path
   that God has chosen for he alone
A man who wants to share his love with someone
   who loves him for the man he is today
I want to be refreshed in the knowledge that
   God's plan for me is simple. To love, to share,
   and bring peace and happiness to all of those
   I love along the way

Too Many Times

I've lost at love too many times
It's never there for me
I've given everything I've had
But never found the we

It seems I always get involved
With those who never find
The kind of love I know exists
And is always on my mind

Yet better to have loved and failed
Then never love again
So I'll keep searching for my love
Until the bitter end

For I know well within my heart
That God has made a plan
And when He feels the time is right
He'll place her in my hand

And if the day should ever come
When the star of love will shine
I'll always be thankful to God up above
Which could never be too many times

Why

Why to fear commitment
  When everything is there
The power to love is frozen
  Inability to share

Try in deepest earnest
  But always ending cold
Begging for completeness
  Before my story's told

Warm and always caring
  Closeness 'til the end
Searching for the lover
  And only finding friends

Something surely missing
  An emptiness of heart
Feelings that were stolen
  When my life was torn apart

I've suffered all the losses
  And groveled in the pain
Help me find my warmth of heart
  And let me love again

For I know I have the caring
  And a soft and tender mind
Please teach me how to love again
  Let me savor the beauty of time

I've Had It

I've had it with the worry
   And the pressure life can bear
I've had it with the sorrow
   From the loves that didn't care
I've had it with the dying
   Of the friends I miss today
I've had it with the loneliness
   Attached to those who stay
I've had it with the fancy cars
   You never seem to own
I've had it with the mortgages
   That really own your home
I've had it with the credit cards
   That never go away
I've had it with the hours of work
   That never let me play
Yet I have the love of children
   And the beauty of the day
I know the hearts of loving friends
   I've met along the way
I've learned to smell the flowers
   And hear the ocean's roar
I've seen the flight of eagles
   As they soar along the shore
I've sensed the snow and tasted rain
   And sailed across the bay
I've held the baby to my chest
   And soothed her tears away
So love your life and live today
   For tomorrow is only a thought
Walk hand in hand, with the Father above
   And enjoy all the blessings He wrought

Love Me As I Am Today

Love me as I am today
   Tomorrow isn't here
Forget the thoughts of yesterday
   And simply hold me near

Love me for the moment now
   For this we truly own
Sense the urgency to care
   For here we're all alone

Discard the thoughts of promises
   That people pledge for years
We've tasted all of that before
   And felt the painful tears

For life is sweet uncertainty
   Bestowed from up above
And worry, hate and jealousy
   Can steal the hours of love

Love me as I am today
   Your true and dearest friend
For if tomorrow never comes
   We're together in the end

My Secret Place

I've always had this secret place
   To shelter me from fear
A haven where I needn't face
   The misery and tears

A pond so hidden in the woods
   Impossible to find
Where quiet waters understood
   My lost and fearful mind

A place where I could wonder
   And try to understand
The thoughts a young boy ponders
   As he tries to find the man

So void of other voices
   Just the wind caressing trees
A place for making choices
   In the life I feared to lead

But like old friends and lovers
   The pond has disappeared
The path is all grown over
   And washed away by years

But even though it's far away
   And never to be seen
My mind is drawn to quiet days
   Where I had the chance to dream

For as the evening sun goes down
   And the birds have ceased to chime
I can always return to the place that I found
   For it lives ever sweet in my mind

The Turtle

The turtle very well could be
   The slowest thing on earth
With shell a little longer
   Than the distance cross its girth

Simply always moving forward
   With intention set in stone
No part of group or heard or pack
   Proudly going it alone

And if he hits an obstacle
   He merely goes around
He doesn't stop to argue
   Just continues to where he's bound

And if he senses danger near
   Vibrations as his guide
He simply draws into his shell
   And awaits the change in tide

For turtles are like people
   With a hardened outer shell
Yet inside beats the softest heart
   Though at times it's hard to tell

So I think I'll emulate his life
   And do the turtle proud
Move with purpose and direction
   Never yielding to the crowd

And when faced with confrontation
 I will merely draw inside
And wait 'til calmer minds prevail
 Like the changing of the tide

And when beset with obstacles
 I'll simply go around
And never stop to waste the time
 That deters from where I'm bound

So if you feel life is agony
 And it's hard to reach your goals
Take a lesson from the turtle
 And the story we've been told

And never forget that famous day
 Or the race beyond compare
For if void of direction and purpose and end
 You may wind up the second place hare

Stay With Me

Stay with me and share the sun
   Walk closely hand and hand
Sense the ever pounding surf
   And warmth of summer sand

Stay with me and sail with me
   As breezes kiss the bay
We'll spend the evenings anchored tight
   Watching sunsets fade away

Stay with me in autumn's chill
   And stroll the wooded lanes
Where trees explode in wondrous hues
   That paint my world again

Stay with me and hold me close
   On hay rides packed with friends
And sing the songs of yesteryear
   Round bonfires at the end

Stay with me in winter's grip
   And snuggle by the fire
Share my love of Christmas time
   And the children so inspired

Stay with me for snowfalls
   That powder all we see
And feel the beauty life beholds
   As you share my eyes with me

Stay with me in spring time
　　Watching landscapes come alive
The budding flowers and greening grass
　　Simply burst before our eyes

Stay with me for Easter time
　　And the thankfulness it holds
At sunrise service on the beach
　　And the glory that unfolds

Stay with me forever more
　　With our hearts entwined as one
Stay with me and hold me near
　　'Til our seasons have all gone

I'll Fly Away

Togetherness the wonder
   Sharing true delight
Yet honor independence
   Or the mind will beckon flight
I'll fly away

Know my dedication well
   Understand my heart
Don't linger on commitment
   That frightens us apart
I'll fly away

Be there for each other now
   For life could be a day
Don't worry for tomorrow
   And the fears of who will stay
I'll fly away

Love me for the moment sweet
   You'll lose it if you fail
Futures are for calendars
   And promises are pale
I'll fly away

So gather all the love you can
   And love the time we share
For tomorrow's yet to happen
   And today is really there
I'll fly away

Please know my heart and listen
    Don't speak of life for years
For nothing yields eternity
    And could all be wasted tears
I'll fly away

So hold me now and understand
    This doesn't mean good-bye
It only means to love yourself
    In this world of you and I
I'll fly away

I Need to Get to Know Me

I need to get to know me
   The introspective soul
The person deep within my mind
   Who shares my growing old

For without the truth of who I am
   And capable to be
My efforts simply wasted time
   As the thoughts of you and me

For a man must learn to love himself
   Before the chance to share
Or risk the pain to someone dear
   From the man who isn't there

For the man that hurts from years of pain
   Still requires the time to heal
To find himself in solitude
   Where he learns he's permitted to feel

And as time passes slowly he learns every day
   And he simply discovers his worth
And deciphers the meaning of living alone
   Finding truth in the self that comes first

And then when he's healed, and the answers are found
   And he's finally ready to share
He can give all the love, that he shared with himself
   As the man who will always be there

Quietness

Quiet is a state of mind
  It's peaceful if you will
It's sensed upon awakening
  In creatures lying still

The total void of movement
  Just the absence so profound
A mirrored pond reflecting
  All the foliage that surrounds

The deafness of the sunrise
  As it lifts above the sea
And softly paints the portrait
  He created just for me

To hold the sleeping baby
  Cradled softly in your arms
Always keeping loving watch
  For the sounds that cause alarm

To hold the hand of someone ill
  Unable to say what they feel
Simply stroking their brow and kissing the cheek
  Words of love that are ever so real

And silence reigns in the eagles' flight
  And the wind that bows the trees
And in the church where silent prayers
  Bring masses to their knees

And as you walk the path of life
  Full of noises and clamor and fear
Remember to quietly listen to God
  As He whispers His love in your ear

Tell Me Why

I wish someone could tell me
   All the things I need to know
The answers never seem to come
   Yet the questions always grow

Why must there be bigotry
   And hearts so full of hate
When everyone is equal
   When they stand at heaven's gate

Any why is there rejection
   For the love we choose to give
When others starve to have the kind
   Of life we long to live

And why do some folks always take
   Never giving in return
And why do people jump the line
   And never wait their turn

And what about the child abuse
   That happens every day
The baby knowing only love
   That's beaten where he lay

And what about the wives of men
   Who torture them with pain
Who only cower and do the deeds
   For fear he'll hurt again

And what about the floods and storms
   And the dying by the score
And earthquakes killing thousands
   In the towns that rise no more

And illness running rampant
   People dying every day
And powerful addictions
   Killing everyone they may

And why must there be murders
   And fatalities of war
And when will peace return to earth
   In a world that hates no more

And though I know these questions
   Are asked by many more
The answer lies in deepest faith
   Of this you must be sure

That everything that God designs
   Is created with an end
And only He can know the time
   To call you home again

That life and all the things you do
   Are firmly in His plan
It's all just going to happen
   Like the tide that steals the sand

Don't worry for the time that's left
   Just be thankful that you're here
It might be only scored in days
   Or maybe thirty years

But know one thing for certain
   That your time will finally come
So face life hand in hand with God
   And be proud of what you've done

My Song

I believe that God has penned
    A song that's just for me
The sharps and flats and notes he writes
    Are my song of life to be

The lyrics he has chosen
    Are the story of my time
And the music placed behind the words
    Will denote the love I find

I know there'll be crescendos
    Full of happiness and glee
And dirges that can fill my heart
    With loss that comes to me

For I am just the instrument
    And God will choose the theme
And only He can set the tone
    To the music of my dream

But most importantly I find
    This song is just for me
There's no duets or choir here
    Just my solo part you see

And never try to play a part
    In another person's song
For theirs is written just for them
    And your notes just don't belong

So listen to your drummer
  And the rhythm that He plays
And know that only He controls
  The song that fills your days

So make your song a happy one
  That's full of love and glee
He writes them just for us alone
  They're his love songs for you and me

In the words of my grade school music teacher written
In my autograph book: "Never B flat, never B sharp,
Always B natural"

My Fantasy

As I sit here alone at fifty-five
    Fifty-six if you will in two days
I can't help but ponder the person I was
    Though he seems to be slipping away

For I've had all the pressure a person can take
    With divorce, money problems and death
I've battled with illness, been sued and been scared
    And have truthfully squeaked by at best

But thanks to my children and a few loving friends
    Who are constantly urging me on
I'm still working and hoping to finally find
    The place where I truly belong

Now working is fine and I'll give it my all
    But the owning and worry must go
I need to be free of the burden I bear
    And just work in the field that I know

Now my fantasy life isn't what you may think
    Doesn't conjure up silver and gold
It's filling my life with the things that I love
    Pleasing others with stories I've told

To be free to write poems of all that I see
    As my life goes on stumbling along
To chronicle thoughts about loving and care
    In a life that seems more like a song

And friends who are close to me know that I ache
　　To be sailing away from the shore
In a little blue boat, called the "Poet" of course
　　And stay out there a few days or more

For out on the water I find all the peace
　　And the solace and beauty and light
To nurture the thoughts and to challenge the mind
　　Just seducing the wonders of life

With God as my captain and faith as my crew
　　It seems I've left nothing to fate
Except for the fact that I'd much rather sail
　　With a loving and beautiful mate

So my fantasy's simple, I don't need a lot
　　My desires are so simple and few
Simply sail through my life, with God and my poems
　　Always loving my wonderful crew

I Never Knew Me

Throughout my fifty something years
    I never knew me well
I thought that I was someone else
    But really couldn't tell

I thought myself successful
    But that would come to pass
For market shares and interest rates
    Would end my thoughts at last

I thought I was a family man
    And sharing all my years
Divorce would turn my life around
    And end my thoughts in tears

I thought that I was many things
    That never came to be
Yet through it all I truly learned
    Another side of me

For from the ashes man can rise
    And sweetly find his soul
The man that always lived inside
    Who now accepts his role

For all the death and tears and loss
    Can cause the heart such pain
Yet all the beauty life beholds
    Can make it sing again

And now my life has meaning
And a purpose to it all
I love to write inspiring words
That help the mind recall

A sweeter time with sunlit days
And starry, starry nights
When love was burning fresh and new
And life was pure delight

But know me well and understand
My life was changed by He
My God who eased the hurt and pain
And lets me smile so free

For only God can show the way
To turn your life around
So walk beside Him hand in hand
And enjoy all the peace that I've found

Downs Syndrome

I believe that God creates
   Some beings just for Him
He wants to see just how much love
   One child can have within

Therefore he made the syndrome
   That we all know as downs
And sprinkled it throughout the world
   Simply spreading love around

When I see these happy kids
   With the beautiful smiling faces
It's easy to see what God has done
   And where He put His graces

For these truly are the children of God
   The chosen and beautiful few
Who go through life, day in, day out
   Full of love for me and you

The thing that really makes me smile
   And I really can't believe
Is how He chose the moms and dads
   Who were worthy to receive

For these are the parents of the children of God
   So patient and loving of heart
And accept all the love that these kids have to give
   And hold it 'til death do they part

The sweetest thing it seems to me
    Is why He put them here
To show us all that love can last
    And last throughout the years

For unlike us these kids grow up
    And still love with the mind of a child
They don't get divorced, or need more space
    They just want to be held for awhile

So if you see a child of God
    Don't feel sad or even forlorn
Simply know that he's one of the few in life
    Who knows why he was born

So stop and chat and listen close
    To what they have to say
They love to laugh and smile and hug
    And always make my day

So God bless the children and parents, too
    And pray that you will know
The kind of love they all receive
    Wherever they may go

So learn to laugh and smile and hug
    And love like these kids do
You'll do very well to follow their path
    Always loving what God gives you

The Poet

The poet is the kind of man
   As you will surely see
That writes of love and flowers and death
   And all the things that be

He often is a man that's hurt
   Or troubled in his time
He uses all his past and love
   To say what's on his mind

He speaks a language all his own
   In a voice that's never loud
He couldn't tell you to your face
   Or say it in a crowd

He writes of hearts and flowers and pain
   And all life has to hold
He speaks of little babies
   And loving the very old

The poet feels and senses things
   You never stop to see
Like storms and suns and skies and love
   All there for you and me

He calls attention to the past
   That life is fleeting by
To take the time to love yourself
   Before the flowers die

He opens his heart and tells it all
　　To each and everyone
He has no fear of what you think
　　Of the work that he has done

For if just one poem, one simple line
　　Can make you stop and smile
Then all the time that he has spent
　　Will make it all worth while

For these are simply stories told
　　A capsule of his strife
He always looks at love and paints
　　The things that make our life

The words just seem to flow right out
　　And keep flowing on for years
He sees life with the kindest heart
　　And even through his tears

To read what he has written
　　Is to truly know him well
But unlike you who keeps it in
　　He's not afraid to tell

For someone has to take the stand
　　To say that life is good
To remind you all to smell the rose
　　And be all the things you would

His loneliness and pain it seems
　　Has cause him to come out
And tell you all the things he loves
　　That's just what he's about

He's not afraid to say what's right
    Or to try to right a wrong
He simply wants you all to think
    And know that you belong

So read what he has written
    Slow down and think awhile
Maybe even shed a tear
    Or crack a little smile

Remember all your days gone by
    Your moments in the sun
That life is just a poet's pen
    And that writing can be fun

So love your life and take the time
    To stop and smell the flowers
'Cause some of them like people, too
    May just be here for hours

So love your friends and family
    Take time to love and care
But if you slip or forget to think
    The poet's always there

The Rising Child

Awaken pure heart, greet the day
    Doff your crown of love
Another day of innocence
    Has come from up above

Put away your dreams for now
    They'll be there in your sleep
For the mind will always recollect
    The ones you dare to keep

For today is not just any day
    It's painted just for you
To learn the wonders life beholds
    In everything you do

Smell the flowers, sense the wind
    Go digging in the sand
Fly the kite on ocean's edge
    Or march behind the band

Repeat the timeless nursery rhymes
    And glean from what you read
For books are penned with wondrous thoughts
    That fill your eager needs

For life is waiting just for you
    It's sweet and full of love
But always remember when kneeling at night
    It's your gift from the Father above

Hate

Now hate is an emotion
    And it's been around for years
It raises up its ugly head
    And brings on shameful tears

Some people hate the job they have
    Or hate the clothes they wear
They hate the restaurant they chose
    And the waiter they can't bear

They hate to be kept waiting
    Yet they hate to move too fast
They hate the lines at movies
    And will scorn the total cast

They're never really happy
    For the hate gets in the way
They can't enjoy the simple things
    That fill each glorious day

But one thing that I've learned in life
    From the people that can hate
They usually do it all alone
    For good friends they never make

So to all you folks who love to hate
    And reject what life can give
Simply try to keep all the hate to yourself
    Let the rest of us love how we live

But if you ever feel you've been left all alone
    Been abandoned by lovers and friends
Simply drop all the hate and replace it with love
    And you'll never be lonely again

The Toilet

If inventions could win the purple heart
    This one goes to Mr. Crapper
For his design has saved our lives
    And surely beats the Clapper

It sits alone in solitude
    Always craving another chance
To see you fly into the room
    And quickly drop your pants

It's here for you so late at night
    When you've had too much to drink
For even though you spray the floor
    It still beats the unflushable sink

It also creates a library air
    Where you quietly study and read
What a marvelous place to read beautiful words
    On the seat where you previously peed

It's the watering hole for the pets in the house
    As they sneak in and lap up a drink
For the height is just perfect for creatures so small
    And another demerit for sinks

It's the place for your foot as you lace up the shoe
    Just another salute to design
And a shelf for the tissues and bottles and junk
    Making toiletries easy to find

So hail to the toilet, the crapper, the head
    It's the bowl of miraculous joy
Only flaw in design, it's a little too tall
    For the peckers of some little boys

Worry

Worry truly seems to be
    The constant gnawing fear
Of what will come or happen next
    As you muddle through the years

There's worry over taxes
    Will I have enough to pay
And worry for the future
    As the years all fade away

There's worry for your children
    Will they have the things they need
And when they're sick or hurting
    Worry magnifies indeed

There's worry when you're all alone
    And need someone to care
For life for me is meant for two
    Worries lessen when you share

There's worry over illness
    That you suffered in the past
The fear it might recur again
    And this time may be the last

Yet as I sit and worry
    For the things I can't control
I still can hear my mentor's voice
    And the lessons I've been told

That God has chosen what will be
    And placed it in my plan
And nothing I can do or say
    Will change the course of man

So learn to listen to His voice
    And hear His words so kind
For love and understanding
    Eases worries of the mind

For worries seem to dissipate
    When love replaces fear
Just trust in God and all He gives
    And the fact He's always near

And know you'll never be alone
    As He's always close by at your side
And travel your path without worry or fear
    Always loving your heavenly guide

Death

It seemed that all throughout my life
    My fear of death had grown
My fear of leaving loved ones
    And the blackness called alone

The horror of those final words
    That you have six months to live
And how you'd face that briefest time
    And the message that you'd give

For everyone would wonder
    How it feels to know the day
When the life we know or think we do
    Would finally fade away

So please believe me when I write
    And how I truly feel
That God is always by my side
    And His love is very real

I know He always holds my hand
    When I walk along the shore
And know He'll hold me in his arms
    When the clock will chime no more

So having faith simply removes all the fear
    Makes the understanding so sweet
So live and be happy and cherish the day
    When the both of you finally will meet

So death needn't be scary or bottled in fears
    For there's always a start and an end
Just always keep loving and caring between
    And you'll finally go home to our Friend

The Rocking Chair

Rocking chairs have been around
    Forever so it seems
Their quiet motion soothes the nerves
    And calms the baby's screams

They're usually in the nursery
    When the little one arrives
And later all throughout the house
    Simply soothing stressful lives

They're found in dens and living rooms
    And placed in kitchens, too
The nicest way to read a book
    While you're waiting for the stew

But as a child my memory
    Drifts to porches on the bay
And the big old dark green rockers
    Where I dreamed my youth away

And our leaders all had rockers
    In the oval office grand
Where rocking gently clears the mind
    For the problems close at hand

So although it seems old fashioned
    Get yourself a rocker soon
The medicine for stress relief
    That keeps your thoughts in tune

And if you have a little one
    Put the child across your chest
And hum the sweetest song you know
    And the rocker will do all the rest

I Remember Sunday Mornings

I remember Sunday mornings
   As I drift across the past
When the honor of the Sabbath
   Was the rule yet fading fast

When all the towns were quiet
   With no access to the stores
And everything you needed
   You would buy the day before

No gas or food or liquor stores
   Available that day
Only churches open wide
   For their flocks to come and pray

And Sunday morning breakfasts
   With everyone in place
And time to eat and talk and share
   Without yielding to the race

And then a shower and off to church
   Where the neighbors all would pray
The cornerstone of Sundays past
   And the meaning for the day

And next the Sunday paper
   That you'd read from end to end
And time to play with children
   Or to visit dearest friends

But Sundays now are memories
    For we're open seven days
Competition raised its ugly head
    Snatched my blessed day away

Now liquor stores and shops and malls
    And supermarkets, too
Have made themselves available
    To better service you

The entire week has been consumed
    With working every day
Many folks have lost the Sabbath
    And the time for family play

The absurdity and irony
    That really makes me sick
If we all would close on Sundays
    We could do it all in six

For God created Heaven and Earth
    Then rested on this day
I think it behooves us to follow his plan
    Lest we're working religion away

To

To love, is sweetest caring
   To care, the act of love
To pray, an act of thankfulness
   To the Father up above

To be, is merely living
   To share, an act for two
To need, is what's required
   To complete the things you do

To smile, an act of kindness
   To grieve, an act of loss
To frown, just causes wrinkles
   To the man who failed the toss

To give, is truly Godly
   To take, is simply mean
To know, is having knowledge
   To enjoy God's wondrous scheme

So if you want To laugh, To smile
   To give, To care, To love
Today could be the place To start
   To speak To God above

To night when kneeling down To pray
   To ask Him To listen To you
To believe is His answer, To be is His gift
   To thine ownself To always be true

Talk to Me

Please talk to me
    You know I'm here
In true anticipation
    The ever trusting ear

Don't wait in hesitation
    For fear of words unsaid
A tome without the pages
    The poem never read

Don't cower from exposure
    The heart must speak its mind
Don't cloak in feigned emotion
    Your feelings veiled with time

Speak into the quiet
    Release the frightened tears
Embrace the loving friendship
    Of the one who knows of fear

Talk to me and understand
    Unspoken fear is pain
And the wall of isolation
    Will allow it to remain

So reach into your warmth of heart
    And let your mind be free
For today could be forever
    And tomorrow might never be

The Lady on the Beach

It happened late September
    After tourists left for home
My favorite time of solitude
    When I had the beach alone

And every crystal evening
    I could walk the unscathed sand
And hear the ocean softly break
    To the rhythm of the land

And the only other sound I heard
    Was the wind that kissed my face
Transporting me so quietly
    To another time and place

And the wonder of the sunset
    That exploded in the west
A canvas splashed with wondrous hues
    That would ease the day to rest

Now on this special evening
    As the day was touching night
A vision came from down the beach
    Like an angel bathed in light

So tall and tan and lovely
    In a filmy gown of white
With barefoot strides so void of thought
    Simply walking into night

And hair that flew in sunset gold
   That breezes pulled to sea
And the sheerest scarf in palest blue
   'Round her neck and standing free

And as she passed beside me
   Always staring out to sea
I saw the face of sadness
   For a love that couldn't be

I know the pain of loneliness
   For I've been there many times
And recognized the tears she wept
   For the love that once was mine

Yet as she left I couldn't help
   But crack the smallest smile
For love can always come again
   Though the heart will be healing awhile

And other sunsets will appear
   More beautiful than before
The ones that only lovers see
   When together on the shore

So every time I walk the beach
   And remember the moment so clear
I squeeze on the hand of my lady beside
   And just whisper my love in her ear

Creation

Creation, the beginning
   First wondrous breath of life
The pinnacle of Godliness
   Unscathed of pain and strife

The birth of hope and innocence
   With a mind untouched and pure
The sweetest blessing God can bring
   To show His love once more

Yet everything you see in life
   All creatures big and small
Are lovingly created
   By the hand that loves us all

All puppies, kittens, fawns and chicks
   And colts and guppies, too
Are all creations of His love
   They're the gifts from God to you

And everything that blossoms
   And grows from year to year
And all the oceans, bays and streams
   We hold in thoughts so dear

Are simply His creations
   All the wonders that He brings
To fill our lives with beauty
   That can make our senses sing

So look around and feel the life
    Created just for you
Be thankful that you have the chance
    To love the things you do

And always hold your family close
    And teach your children well
And speak of God and all His love
    In the stories that you tell

For our children are truly creations of God
    And the reason He caused us to be
So always remember to teach them to love
    And to savor the gifts that they see

The Lighthouse

There's a lighthouse standing proudly
    On the rocky barren shore
With shafts of light that stab the sea
    Above the ocean's roar

It's a warning and a welcome
    To everyone at sea
The landfall you've been searching for
    Has finally come to be

Be careful 'round the rocks and shoals
    And bless your journey home
And though you sail in solitude
    You're truly not alone

For the other little lighthouse
    Is tended with great care
The one that sends a beam of love
    To show you that He's there

So if you're ever lost in life
    And just can't find your way
Look to God and find the light
    That brightens every day

And when you reach the lighthouse
    That calls to heaven's door
The Keeper stands with open arms
    To bring you home once more

The Past Gets in the Way

Sometimes the past gets in the way
   And stifles all your dreams
It holds the future well at bay
   Life's jailer so it seems

It's all the things we thought we were
   And times we thought would last
And even though they're gone away
   Some folks just can't get passed

They stay involved with life gone by
   And simply can't move on
Stagnation in a life of pain
   They've known so very long

But one day soon the time will come
   When recognition starts
You'll know it's time to move ahead
   To see what life imparts

But until then you'll never know
   What happiness can do
So put away the yesterdays
   And find the new born you

Shooting Stars

Sometimes in summer evenings
    After sunset turns to night
I love to lie upon my back
    And ponder heaven's light

In sky that turns to darkest blue
    Unscathed by light of moon
The sparklers all appear once more
    To light the evening gloom

And most of all I love to watch
    The shooting stars go by
That streak across the universe
    So wondrous as they die

For each and every one of us
    Is simply a beautiful star
That God has placed upon this earth
    To share all the love that we are

For every sunrise stars will fade
    And people will slowly rise
We simply take the place of those
    Who dance in the evening sky

And one thing to remember well
    As you shine throughout the year
Sense all the beauty life truly beholds
    And savor it all without fear

And when your time has finally come
    To go home to the Father above
Streak through the sky with a smile in your heart
    For you've finished a lifetime of love

GOD

Many people have a thought
   Of what their God should be
Most of them are frightened
   Of the power that is He

Many only pray to Him
   When troubled or afraid
They fear the retribution
   For the sins that they have made

But this I never understand
   For that's not the God I know
Mine just imparts forgiveness
   And doesn't strike a blow

For I believe that I was born
   With purity and love
Created in His image
   With the blessing from above

I believe it is my function
   To live my life the way
This Godliness intended me
   To greet each glorious day

By caring for the people
   That filter through my life
And always try to find a way
   To ease their pain and strife

For helping others seems to be
    The only loving way
To show my God I have the heart
    To lighten someone's day

So if you truly do believe
    And know He's in your heart
Emulate Him in your thoughts
    And you'll never be apart

For He is with you every day
    And lets you make the call
Permits mistakes and even sins
    Yet forgives you after all

So if you slip or even fall
    Please never cower in fear
Because our God forgives all sins
    And will always hold you near

At Fifty-Six

At fifty-six the time has come
　To strip the closet clean
And rid myself of all the things
　I've owned, but never seen

It's time to taste the soul of life
　The reason that we're here
To feel the earth and smell the wind
　I've missed in recent years

To sweetly walk the lonely beach
　And sing above the roar
And lie upon the sun drenched sand
　Like the boy I knew before

To put away the thoughts of wealth
　That only lives today
And take the time to savor life
　Before it slips away

At fifty-six I've seen it all
　Whatever that might be
But never stopped to truly sense
　The wonder that was me

For God created me to love
　The wonders that He brings
From mountains high, to flowers sweet
　And birds that softly sing

To feel the grass beneath my feet
And sense the warmth of sun
And feel the pulse of natures' song
The tune that's played for one

So ease the pressure, take the time
And throw away the pain
At fifty-six the clock is fast
And you'll never rewind it again

Born to Love

It's hard for me to pen the words
   To tell you how I feel
For I know I was born to love
   With passion ever real

I love the things that God has wrought
   From trees to fields and streams
And love to walk the beach at night
   With one who shares my dreams

I love to watch the sun explode
   At sunrise o'er the sea
And see the sunset painted gold
   God's gift of love to thee

I love to watch my daughters grow
   As women wise and strong
And love to hug their little ones
   Who always tag along

I love to help the older folks
   Who love you in return
And love to listen to their tales
   And love the need to learn

But most of all I love my life
   And love the one I hold
For loving doesn't fade with time
   It lasts as one grows old

And though we wrinkle, bend and tire
   And shuffle as we may
I'll always love you 'til the end
   Just as much as I love you today

Sweet Nothings

The sweetest little nothings
  Extracted from the heart
Whispered in the softest tones
  Loves' beautiful remarks

Breathless words unfounded
  Meanings always known
Words that say I love you
  And you'll never be alone

Phrases meant to kiss you
  And hold you in the night
With wondrous expectations
  That you'll share the morning light

So though we call them nothings
  They're everything you see
They're words that touch the sweetest heart
  And hold it close to thee

So if you truly are in love
  Speak nothings every day
And always know that nothings count
  When you give your heart away

Rise Above the Pain

I try to rise above the pain
   That's saddled me for years
The pain of losing one you love
   Through arguments and tears

I try to rise above the pain
   As love ones slowly die
And felt the pangs of helplessness
   To watch the moments fly

I try to rise above the pain
   Of being all alone
No one to speak to, touch or hold
   The loneliness of home

I try to rise above the pain
   And now I feel I may
For God has come to walk with me
   And light my darkened day

And now I stand above the pain
   Walk beaches with a smile
For one thing now I understand
   He's been with me all the while

My Guardian Angel

This poem is a confession
  Of what I truly feel
I know I have an angel
  Standing by me, and she's real

Now you may think I'm crazy
  But I really just don't care
For I'm the lucky one to have
  This lady watching there

Now you may ask just how I know
  This angel is a she
I wish that I could tell you
  But that's for God and me

He put her here beside me
  And she always holds me near
To help me down the path of life
  Throughout these trying years

I know she's always in my mind
  She's always in my love
She fills my heart with wondrous thoughts
  That come from up above

Whenever I am tired or lost
  Or feel I cannot cope
She redirects my thoughts in life
  And gives me added hope

She's been there for me many times
   In crisis so it seems
And always watching over me
   As I pursue my dreams

I had my closest brush with death
   In nineteen eighty-two
And once again she held my hand
   And helped me make it through

I've dealt with death and all its pain
   Divorce and illness too
And yet I seem to rise again
   And face my life renewed

For only she knows when it's time
   For me to sweetly die
And until then she knows I'll rise
   To give another try

For angels come the day you're born
   And stay until you die
To smile upon you when you laugh
   Or hold you when you cry

To keep you safe until the day
   It's time to take you home
But 'til that day, remember friend
   You'll never be alone

Alone in a Crowd

Have you ever been to parties
    And truly felt alone
Where wasted words and plastic smiles
    Have truly set the tone

And feel you simply don't belong
    And can't imagine why
And though you feel you need to fit
    You never even try

You simply watch the clock and hope
    The time will quickly fade
And graciously you'll take your leave
    With no attention paid

For this is what I feel in life
    Most times I don't belong
And though we all have felt this way
    For me it's very strong

For life to me is very real
    I taste it every day
I smell the flowers, walk the sand
    And love my life away

I dream of beauty far beyond
    The parties and the gold
The wonder of the crashing waves
    And greatest books of old

The beauty of the painting
   And the magic of the song
The majesty of redwood trees
   So powerful and strong

The sweetness of the little child
   And lovers hand in hand
The wonder of the sunrise bold
   And lightning cross the land

So mingling with the masses
   Is difficult at best
I'd rather sense creation now
   Let imitation rest

For life is filled with wondrous things
   Created just for you
So skip the party, walk the beach
   And sense His gift to you

Oh How I Love The Child In Me

Oh how I love the child in me
   I'm so happy that he's there
The boy who lets me savor life
   And remembers how to share

Oh how I love the child in me
   Who loves to sing out loud
Who's not afraid to laugh at life
   And stands above the crowd

Oh how I love the child in me
   Who's not afraid to dream
And still believes the future holds
   The best of what we've seen

Oh how I love the child in me
   Who pushes back the pain
Reminds me what it is to dance
   And frolic in the rain

For in the heart of every man
   There lurks a little boy
The one that always knew of hope
   When every day was joy

When life was kites and butterflies
   And swimming at the lake
And fishing holes and camping trips
   All memories we'd make

Oh how I love the child in me
And pray he's always there
To wonder at the sunsets bold
And never cease to care

Oh how I love the child in me
And will until the end
For God made the child, that still lives in my heart
And He'll hold us forever as friends

Follow The Leader

Follow the leader is most people's creed
    If it's working for him then I'll follow his lead
I'll never need answers to questions I had
    I just copy the champion, for good or for bad
I won't even strive for a mind of my own
    I'll just go through the actions the leader condones
And everyone knows if the leader succeeds
    The ones that shall follow will meet all their needs

But this never works for a mind that is free
    Who would truly prefer to be all he can be
Who stands on his own in the maddening crowd
    And makes his decisions, though never out loud
He quietly measures the path that he'll choose
    And follows his senses, not fearing to lose
For this is a man with a mind of his own
    Who lives with the answers he garnered alone

So if you long for leaders to take you through life
    I suggest you try God and a wonderful wife
For God is the answer to all that we know
    And is always beside you where ever you go
Who's always been with you in trouble or fears
    And held you in darkness, in pain or in tears
So follow the leader who's given you life
    And share all His love with a wonderful wife

Be Gentle With Yourself Today

Be gentle with yourself today
   Don't startle birds to flight
Enjoy the peace and solitude
   As sunsets turn to night

Be gentle with yourself today
   And feel your soul at ease
Release the fears of yesterday
   And savor all you please

Be gentle with yourself today
   And let your heart run free
For love will once again return
   And brighten all you see

Be gentle with yourself today
   And always wear a smile
For God is with you hand in hand
   And holds you all the while

I'm So Happy At The Bottom

I'm so happy at the bottom
   Of the barrel as they say
And though it took me several years
   I just arrived today

My money's all been stripped away
   My home and assets too
My credit's quite appalling
   And I'm all alone like you

Survival's now become the word
   Existence is my creed
And everything I make today
   Is merely filling needs

Divorce has taken all the things
   That most will never know
It stole the joy together brings
   And trashed the will to grow

For now my life is nothingness
   At least it may appear
Yet every day must have a dawn
   And mine shall rise this year

I'm so happy at the bottom
   For there's nothing more to steal
And finding God along the way
   Has made my life more real

I finally learned at fifty-six
   It isn't what you own
It's not the cars and bank accounts
   That yields a happy home

I'm so happy at the bottom
   For it signifies the start
Another chance to rise again
   And taste what life imparts

I'm so happy at the bottom
   For there's one thing that no one can take
The love in my heart for the ones I hold dear
   And the mark that I'm going to make

I Once Met A Man

I once met a man, who didn't have hands
Yet he smiled every day, because life was so grand

I once met a man, who didn't have arms
Yet he laughed as he told me the funniest yarns

I once met a man, who didn't have feet
Yet the sound of his cello was ever so sweet

I once met a man, who didn't have eyes
Yet his sculpture in clay was a wondrous surprise

I once met a man, who didn't know God
And we all felt sorry for his loss

My Friend John

John my strong and crusty friend
   The toughest of them all
He faced his life as running back
   And never dropped the ball

He lived through all the hurt and pain
   That others seldom feel
Yet never stopped to lick his wounds
   That truly never healed

He fought his way through alcohol
   Victorious again
And faced divorce and cancer too
   My ever fearless friend

The champion of the football field
   The man on the diving horse
The guy who took a swing at life
   And seldom felt remorse

But mostly as I wander back
   To think about my friend
The loss of being by his side
   Will haunt me 'til the end

For John was always there for me
   Through all my pain and tears
My mentor and my friend for life
   That understood my fears

And though appearing tough and gnarled
 His heart was filled with love
And even though he's passed away
 I sense him up above

And as I sail or walk the beach
 Or watch as sunsets fade
The thoughts of John are always there
 And all the plans we made

And as the evening wind subsides
 In a whisper I quietly hear
A voice saying sweetly, "I still love ya pal"
 And I smile for the love in my tears

Mother

Mother, God's creative best
　The paramount of love
The one who filled my mind and heart
　With goodness from above

Mother, always there for me
　To soothe the hurt and pain
To wipe the tears and hold me close
　While never casting blame

Mother, always filled with pride
　With everything I do
My mentor, friend and confidant
　That helped me make it through

Mother, always by my side
　Unquestioned in her faith
Who faced life hand in hand with God
　This lady full of grace

Mother, though she's gone from me
　I know she's always there
She's held me in my loneliness
　When life was pure despair

Mother, though it's several years
　Since God has called you home
I still can hear your wondrous laugh
　And know I'm not alone

Mother, this is just for you
　　Your poem filled with love
That reaches out through time and space
　　To kiss you up above

Mother, always in my heart
　　And ever in my mind
Until the day, the boy straggles home
　　To the arms of his mother, divine

Notice To The Reader

The last six poems were written for six beautiful women, who constantly urged me to publish my poems. They are my cheerleaders and friends, and without their devotion this book would have never been published. I love them dearly.

Julie

This poem is for my daughter
   The eldest of the two
The loving wife and mother
   So devoted to her crew

The one with all the energy
   That blazes through the day
With kids that hang all over her
   And hug her as they may

So full of sensitivity
   She cares for all she sees
This child of love and tenderness
   That always fights to please

She's faced sincere adversity
   And always passed the test
She made the choices just for her
   That proved to be the best

But I always see the baby
   That I rocked away to sleep
That little toe head, full of love
   That smiled in slumber deep

I see her playing soccer
   Or catching at the plate
Or see her laughing down the halls
   With all the friends she'd make

But mostly I remember
    And pray that she will too
The times we spent together
    And the laughter that ensued

We've shared a lot throughout our lives
    The smiling and the tears
Yet always held each others' hand
    And will for many years

So Julie this is just for you
    A poem to remember my love
For a father and daughter with love such as ours
    Is a blessing that's sent from above

I love you Julie, Dad

Stacey

This poem is being written
 For the youngest of the clan
The one I work with every day
 And tolerates my plan

She's been beside me through it all
 My mentor ever strong
She always tells me where to go
 And where I don't belong

We share each others' hopes and dreams
 The laughter and the tears
And understand each others' hearts
 And calm each others' fears

But mostly I remember
 As I wander in the past
A skinny kid with pigtails
 Yet with beauty that would last

I see her with her people
 And a joy you can't replace
I see her on the soccer field
 Or protecting second base

I see her running down the beach
 With pigtails in the wind
Or digging in the sand for hours
 The quiet Stacey Lynn

In December she'll be married
  It's the perfect time of year
For Stacey truly emulates
  The warmth of Christmas dear

We've been together for many years
  My sweet and trusted friend
We've walked together hand and hand
  And will until the end

I only hope and pray my child
  That God will be so kind
To let me see your house of kids
  That's ever on your mind

For no matter where life takes me
  You're always in my heart
For memories linger forever
  And we truly are never apart

So Stacey remember, and never forget
  All the love you were privileged to see
For a father and daughter with love such as ours
  Is the theme for your children to be

I love you Stacey, Dad

Aunt Laura

This poem is written with all the love
    That my heart is able to write
To speak of this lady so close to my soul
    Is like taking a walk in the light

For she truly is wisdom and sweetness and love
    And is always living her song
She knows what to say and heal all my pain
    As my life goes stumbling on

When I lost my mother it seemed like my world
    Had suddenly stopped in its tracks
My marriage in trouble, my business was bad
    And my mentor was not coming back

But there was Aunt Laura, standing right by my side
    Always soothing and pushing me on
To a much better place and a happier heart
    So the heartache was finally gone

She taught me that God lives right in my soul
    Which brought so much comfort to me
And with all of the love that I hold in my heart
    I could challenge the future you see

Because love is the answer and God is my love
    As I walk down this path we call life
And finally happiness entered my world
    And ended my sorrow and strife

She just can't imagine what impact she's had
    On what once was a pitiful soul
And all that she taught me and how I now stand
    As a man who has taken control

For my life was a wreck, always scary and tough
    But she taught me to take it in stride
And to follow my heart as I always had done
    Keeping Christ on my side as my guide

When we say that we love someone dear to our heart
    But we can't find the right words to use
I simply say Laura, that's my word for love
    It's a feeling I never will lose

She's a beautiful lady, an artist and friend
    Seeing beauty in life every day
And I always will hold her deep in my heart
    As my years all go drifting away

For she is the spirit in all that I do
    In my feeling, my loving, my care
And she knows in her heart that as long as I live
    That for her I will always be there

I just wanted to thank her for all that she's done
    And simply feel sorry for you
For if you had a Laura as part of your life
    You would be a much happier you

                        Thank You
                        Love Joe

Mary

I have this friend I'm proud to say
    Who's little and petite
I found her just a few years back
    When God thought we should meet

She came to me in worst of times
    As angels do it seems
To have someone that understands
    And listens to my dreams

She's seen what life is all about
    She's lived with all the pain
But knows the beauty life beholds
    And how to start again

For each day to her is precious
    Just as it is to me
She taught me how to love my life
    And laugh at what I see

She took the role, a dangerous part
    Most people couldn't do
To be my very dearest friend
    And love my ex-wife too

Yet both my wife and I each know
    That everything we say
Will stay with Mary, held in trust
    And never to betray

I always wonder how God knows
    When it seems the time is right
To come to you, reach out to you
    Put a Mary in your life

For she must know I'm thankful
    To have her by my side
I'll always keep her close to me
    My soul mate and my guide

Mary, words can't tell you
    How much you mean to me
I tried to write this little poem
    But it's not enough you see

To tell you how I love your heart
    And how I hold you dear
I only hope it's in God's plan
    We'll be friends for years and years

                    Love Joe

Betty

I meet so many women
   As my life goes fleeting by
Some I dare remember
   And others I never try

Yet it never fails to happen
   When it's least expected to
That someone walks into your life
   As beautiful as you

I remember the day so very well
   When I came into your home
And saw you walking down the stairs
   So regal and alone

And as Mary introduced us
   It was quick for me to see
That we would spend some time alone
   Just chatting you and me

It always seems amazing
   That true beauty knows no time
It's given out to just a few
   Like sweet words put to rhyme

To see a woman at your age
   Who still lights up a room
Just proves that beauty's ageless
   Like the sun and stars and moon

Sitting with you on the stairs
   Was truly a delight
Your kindness warmth and humor
   Gave me quite a lovely night

I felt so very welcome
   Like an old and trusted friend
And you seemed to sense just where I was
   A reject on the mend

So I guess I'm simply writing
   To say I'm always there
If you need someone to talk to
   That truly likes to share

So if you just pick up the phone
   To merely say hello
It's nice to have another friend
   When feeling sad or low

And always know within your heart
   That God is always near
To lift us up on blue gray days
   And fill our hearts with cheer

It's wonderful to be alive
   Watch sunsets, trees and flowers
And just be thankful for the day
   That sweetly clocks in hours

Today's your day, it's just for you
   So give your best to try
It's like no other one before
   It's made for you and I

So listen to me closely dear
   For this I know is true
God has given me a friend
   And I'd like to call her you

              Love Joe

Aunt Mary

I met Aunt Mary a few years back
   While shopping at the store
The sweetest smile and kindest words
   This lady I truly adore

She always holds my hand in hers
   While speaking to my face
Always simply caring words
   And never in a race

I see her every now and then
   We always seem to meet
And running into her each time
   Became my special treat

She exemplifies the good in life
   The way we all should be
And if I had her calmness now
   I'd be a better me

She loves to laugh and always smiles
   With a twinkle in her eye
She tells she really knows of life
   And love that never dies

She's all I ever hope to be
   So loving and sincere
I want to keep her close to me
   This friend I hold so dear

And now each time I see her car
        She parks across the street
I grab my coat and hustle out
        On one more chance we'll meet

Because she makes me feel so good
        She really makes my day
For when I get my little hug
        My worries fade away

And though I'll fall in love again
        May even take a wife
Aunt Mary's still my medicine
        The tonic to my life

So this I pledge to everyone
        And I say it all with pride
The reason I can love again
        I have Aunt Mary on the side

                            Love Joe

"Becalmed... To be without wind, without waves, to be still. I think I want to... Becalmed!"

Joseph Hoey